Couple Therapy Book

SOLVING COUPLE QUALMS

The Decisive Book To Resolve Conflicts In Relationships

WAYNE WEST

Table of Contents

Chapter 1: *Stop Setting Unrealistic Expectations of Your Partner* 6

Chapter 2: 9 Ways to Achieve Harmony In Your Professional Relationships 9

Chapter 3: **9 Signs of a Toxic Relationship** 14

Chapter 4: How To Be A Better Listener 19

Chapter 5: How To Deal With Feeling Anxious In A Relationship 23

Chapter 6: 6 Signs You Need To Give Yourself Some Personal Space 25

Chapter 7: *6 Ways To Deal With Arguments In A Relationship* 29

Chapter 8: *What To Do When You Have Thoughts of Breaking Up* 33

Chapter 9: 8 Signs That Someone Is Not Your Soulmate 36

Chapter 10: *Make Time for Your Partner* 40

Chapter 11: 7 Ways To Live Together In Harmony With Your Partner 43

Chapter 12: *7 Ways To Deal With An Overly Jealous Partner* 47

Chapter 13: Learning To Trust Others 51

Chapter 14: Dealing With Money in Relationships 54

Chapter 15: Feeling Insecure In Your Relationship 57

Chapter 16: What to Do When You Are At Different Life Stages In A Relationship 60

Chapter 17: Don't Overthink Things 64

Chapter 18: Dealing with Abuse in Relationship 66

Chapter 19: Being Authentic 69

Chapter 20: 7 Reasons Why Men Cheat 72

Chapter 21: *What Happens When You Get Bored In A Relationship* 76

Chapter 22: 6 Ways to Stay Committed in a Relationship 79

Chapter 23: Being 100% Happy Is Overrated 83

Chapter 24: *6 Signs Your Love Is One Sided* 86

Chapter 25: How To Worry Less 90

Chapter 26: Don't Make Life Harder Than It Needs To Be 94
Chapter 27: 10 Thoughts That Can Destroy Relationships 98
Chapter 28: *7 Ways To Attract Happiness* 103
Chapter 29: 8 Ways To Gain Self-Confidence 107
Chapter 30: 8 Ways To Love Yourself First 111
Chapter 31: 9 Tips on How To Have A Strong Relationship............. 116

Chapter 1:
Stop Setting Unrealistic Expectations of Your Partner

Are you wondering how to stop unmet expectations from ruining your relationship? Do you find yourself constantly disappointed with your partner and thinking about ending it?

There are ways to stop unmet expectations from ruining your relationship. Here are a few.

1. Identify Your Own

One way to stop unmet expectations from ruining your relationship is by questioning your own. What do you think you need from your partner? Do you need him to give up his friends and hobbies for you? Do you expect to have sex every night? Do you want her to keep the house spotlessly clean as your mother did? Do you expect him to anticipate your every need?

Expectations like these are exactly the things that can kill a relationship. I would encourage you to think about what you want from your partner so that it's clear in your mind. I also want you to consider if your expectations are reasonable.

If your expectations aren't reasonable, your relationship might be dead upon arrival. If you don't know your expectations, your partner will have a hard time reaching them because you might always be moving the goal post. So, before unmet expectations destroy your relationship, make sure you know what yours are.

2. Set Boundaries

I always encourage new couples to set boundaries in their relationships as soon as possible To understand healthy relationship boundaries, look at the four walls of your house. Those walls are the structure that holds your life together. They hold your food and your bed and your possessions, and it's where you live your life.

Healthy boundaries are the same as those four walls of your house. They are the things that support your relationship as it matures. To have a healthy relationship that can grow and be fruitful, it must have structures and boundaries that support it. Healthy boundaries come in many shapes, sizes, and colors.

A few examples:

- Make sure you stay yourself
- Allow yourselves time apart
- Communication is important
- Mutual respect at all times

- Keep the power dynamic equal
- Making time for both sides of the family
- Respecting others friends and hobbies

Of course, each couple needs to decide what works for them, but every couple must establish some boundaries early and stick to them for the sake of their relationship.

3. Be Truthful

You must discuss this with your partner if your expectations aren't being met. One of the most common complaints that I hear from women is 'he should know what I need. I shouldn't have to tell him.' And this, I am afraid, is mostly impossible. Men would love to anticipate and meet our needs, but many of them just don't always have it in them. This is not some deficiency of character but because men have no idea how women think and why. It's a mystery to them, so expecting them to be able to do so will set you up for disaster.

Chapter 2:
9 Ways to Achieve Harmony In Your Professional Relationships

Offices are a microcosm of humanity. They are a mix of all types of people, with all types of personalities, quirks, goals, and challenges, so for everyone to get along beautifully, it takes effort.

You probably remember a time in your career when a "clash of personalities" corrupted a productive working environment. You can prevent this from happening and create harmony in your office with these nine simple practices.

1. Say Thank You

These two little words may be the most powerful when it comes to creating happiness and harmony. People work hard and take pride in their accomplishments but can feel overlooked. Taking time to acknowledge even the smallest achievement can make a person feel valued. Say thank you not only for the big job they've completed, say thank you when they open the door, offer to get you coffee or invite you to lunch. Offer a genuine thank you every day.

2. Notice The Little Things

If a co-worker or employee is happy at their job, they will go out of their way to add a little extra to their commitment. They might take on an extra assignment or stay late to help out with an uncompleted project. Or they may do subtle things like clean up the kitchen area or edit a company document on which they noticed errors. The more you notice and offer thanks for these little "extras," the more you will build happiness and harmony in the office, and the more motivated your co-workers will become to continue looking for ways to improve the business.

3. Avoid Idle Gossip

Gossip can tarnish office harmony. It might seem entertaining at the moment, but underneath, it builds distrust. Resentments build, people begin to wonder if they are the ones being gossiped about, and chasms open. Establish a "no-gossip policy" and enforce it. Extend your no-gossip policy for events outside the office as well, such as happy hours, company outings, or holiday parties, where relaxed environments and alcohol can loosen inhibitions.

4. Maintain An Open-Door Policy

Establish an open environment for discussion by creating a "come to me anytime" system. Be open to suggestions, complaints, or discussions without judgment. Because people come from different backgrounds and experiences, everyone has their way of looking at things. By listening, you can understand what others see from their point of view instead of your own. When people feel open to talk, you can nip problems in the bud before they escalate into real obstacles or unearth substantial opportunities you may not have noticed before.

5. Create A Team Environment

Hold regular meetings with the entire office and empower co-workers to take "ownership" of the business. If they feel their opinions and insights hold value, they will be more likely to use their talents and creativity to help build the business as a whole. Instead of taking orders, they will work together to look for ways to improve.

6. Offer To Help

Jump in and be hands-on yourself. Whenever you are stuck, overworked, or faced with a major deadline, you know how you appreciate a helping hand. It may take a little extra effort, but pitch in to help your co-workers over a hump.

7. Socialize Outside Of Work

Build friendships and harmonies outside of work with casual outings. Plan a monthly happy hour, establish a yearly barbeque picnic or kick up a friendly competition with a bowling or softball tournament. The relaxed environment will create bonds that go deeper than the company's latest accounting policies.

8. Get Everyone Involved

Every employee likes to be informed and in the loop, even if the news has nothing to do with them. Keeping an employee informed is an effortless way to make them feel appreciated and valuable in your business. Beyond this, you should always trust your team and be confident in delegating work to them – nobody likes working under a boss who micromanages everything they do and gives them no individuality in their work. Getting everyone involved is an easy way to please even the lowest-level employees and ensure that your office has harmony.

9. Communicate

Communication is crucial for any work environment. Every boss needs to have an open-door policy and be willing to talk to an employee at any time; on the other hand, every employee needs to be sure that they reach out and talk to higher-level employees. Learning is crucial in any office, and the central way for workers to learn is through communication. Beyond communication about work, occasional non-work-related talk is also important – it's a bad sign if you don't know anything about your fellow worker outside of work. Ask someone about their family or hobbies or whatever it may be; these small talk conversations may seem meaningless but are important for building harmony in the workplace.

Chapter 3:
9 Signs of a Toxic Relationship

Before getting into the video, let's talk about what's a toxic relationship? Dr. Lillian Glass, a California-based psychology expert defines the toxic relationship as "any relationship [between two people who] don't support each other, where there's conflict and one seeks to undermine the other, where there's competition, where there's disrespect and a lack of cohesiveness."

Signs of toxic relationships are all around us. The question is how do we know if we have one? And what are the exact signs of such a relationship? In this video, I'm going to tell you 9 main signs of a toxic relationship. So let's get right into it.

Main

1. Unhealthy Communication Patterns

Passive aggressiveness, aggressive or bullying styles of conversations that your partner engages with you could be a clear sign that something isn't right between the two of you. The relationship can turn toxic very quickly when either partner feels guilted into responding in a submissive way to please the other. Furthermore bad communication can also lead to avoiding talking to your partner. Instead of treating you with love and compassion, if your partner has animosity, criticism, sarcasm, and egoism in most of his conversations with you, then it can lead to hatred and thus poison the relationship. We all want a partner who can speak to us with kindness and understanding rather than someone who speaks to us in a threat-like manner.

2. Habits or Cycles of Cheating and lying

If you feel that your partner is cheating on you or lying to you, it will damage your trust in your partner and may also harm the relationship. Once trust is lost, it is very difficult to get it back. You may start to trust your partner in days or months, but the possibility always seems fragile. Relationships with distrust can turn good partners into jealous or suspicious people. Sometimes even your partner's unforgettable compromises can't repair trust if it is badly broken. So, if for some reason you can't trust your partner then the relationship is definitely toxic.

3. Your Loved Ones Strongly Disapproves of Your Partner

What people close to you think of your partner is one of the most important factors in determining whether the relationship is beneficial or one that could be toxic. So, make sure to pay close attention to what your friends, family, and loved ones are saying about your partner.

Your family and friends always want you to be safe and happy, so if they strongly dislike your partner then there must be a strong reason behind it. They may be able to see red flags in them that you might have otherwise overlooked that may point towards something toxic brewing. That reason or some hateful reactions of your loved ones against your partner can indicate that the relationship is not good for you.

4.   Over-Dependency On Your Partner

It has been noted by several personality experts that those who are the least self-sufficient (but also most self-critical) tend to be the most toxic partners. Sometimes this is a symptom of an underlying relationship problem. Sometimes it is not. But when a partner is absent-minded or disinterested in "self-care", that can be a red flag.

5.   Constant Fears of Being Judged

Signs of toxic relationships can also include the feeling like you are constantly being judged. You may wonder why you always feel like you need to be on your best behavior. Or, you may think that you always get in trouble with your partner. Some partners can even pick fights as a way of getting back at their relationship - and then some feel like nothing's ever going right.

6.   Feeling like you are being taken advantage of

One of the most important signs of toxic relationship behavior is feeling like you're being exploited. You may feel like you're not really treated with care or value. Perhaps you question whether or not you are important enough. You may worry that your partner sees you as someone they can take for granted.

In fact, one of the core dynamics of toxic relationships is that the less valuable you feel, the less valuable your partner will feel. When you have a deep, internal belief that you are not significant, it can lead to behaviors that are meant to hurt you.

7. You Are Always Defending Your Partner

One classic sign of toxic relationship behavior is when you find yourself defending your partner against charges of hurting you or you feel guilty and always come first to apologize to your partner but you are not sure why.

When the lines of communication between you and your partner start to break down, you may find yourself defending your partner instead of talking to solve problems. When you and your partner argue, you may also hear your partner say things like "you just need to learn to get along with people," "your problem is with you, not with me" or "you just want to ruin my life." Such behavior is enough to call the relationship toxic.

8. All the compromise comes from you

Nobody can manage a good relationship with a partner if they are the only one doing all compromise, work, and love.

A good relationship can only be built with the cooperation of both life partners. However, if you do everything while your partner does nothing and never gives the relationship a better chance to improve, then, of course, the relationship is toxic to you.

9. Your Partner Suffers From Addictions

The use of drugs, especially alcohol or (maybe) cigarettes, has a devastating effect on all relationships and is a major reason for leaving relationships. If your partner is addicted to drugs, and you think you can't solve the problem then make sure to provide him/her medical help.
But if he/she is not ready at all to get rid of drugs and drinks too much alcohol regularly, you should consider the relationship toxic.

Closing
So that's it. We are done with our today's topic.

Remember that if you feel that you are in a toxic relationship, don't forget to seek help. Consult your friends and family, be open to their opinions and don't be afraid to end the relationship if it indeed turns out to be toxic. Remember that we only have one life to live and we deserve to be with a partner that can care and love us unconditionally in all the right ways.

Now it's your turn to share your thoughts. Do you know about any other signs of a toxic relationship? Let us know in the comments below. If you got value then hit the like and subscribe button.

Chapter 4:
How To Be A Better Listener

Today we're going to talk about a topic that could potentially help you not only in your relationships, such as with your boyfriend, girlfriend, and best friends, but also in your workplace with your colleagues, peers, and your bosses or understudies.

Why is being a better listener so vital you might ask? It is simple, because as humans, we all want to be heard. And we all want to feel like people are listening to us and understanding us not just on a superficial level, but emotionally as well. We have a desire to share our pains, sorrows, unhappiness, and even happiness and special events with people who are willing to lend a listening ear to us. And we instantly feel connected to the person who is listening to us.

We are given a mouth and two ears for a reason. I know it sounds silly, but I have to repeat again here that we are social creatures, and we try to find connections with people as much as we can. And there is no better way to be connected than with someone who are willing to spend the time to hear us.

Think back to a time when someone actually told u, thanks for listening to my problems. Either through text or in person. How did you feel? And how did they react to you being a good listener? Were they appreciative? Or were they nonchalant about it. I would bet that they were appreciative and they know that they had found someone that they could count on to tell their problems too. Of course u dont want it to be a habit that someone constantly "bitches" to you about every single thing that is going wrong in their life. You have to learn how to draw the line there. But generally if it is a one-off problem, I'm sure you guys became better friends, partners, or lovers.

Now think back to a time when someone told u off for not listening to their problems. Where you constantly interjected their sharing with advice without letting them finish what they had to say. This would most likely be your partner who would get angry at you, but what were their feelings at that point? Did they say "you're not listening to me" or "You dont understand?". That has happened to me before on multiple occasions when i tried to impose my ideas on a situation thinking that that is what the person wanted, advice. But in reality, they know how to solve the problem but they just want someone that they could vent to. To share their story and then move on.

So if people have been telling u that you're not a good listener, or that you don't listen or that u dont understand what they want, more often than not, the problem is that you did not just let the person say what they wanted to say, to have their piece. Your job is not to dish out advice, but just to sit there, interested, and ask them to go on. And at the end of it give out a hug rather than an advice.

So you must be wondering how this could link to your colleagues. Well for one, you have to be a good person to begin with in order for people to trust u with work related matters. If colleagues don't trust you, they won't be open to sharing with you problems they might have with their bosses or other issues that they need to vent about. But if they do trust you, and know you are not the type who will go round spreading gossip but rather is a good genuine person with a good heart and a listening ear, you have just gotten yourself an ally at the workplace. And you would have built a friendship at work that could last you a lifetime. You never know when these connections that you have made would provide you with future job opportunities, whether these colleagues could become your bosses in another company one day. But you want to keep your colleagues close to you and you want to retain their respect, trust, and be professional. Vice versa, you may also find a listening ear in a colleague that you can share your problems with. But i must warn you that sometimes people can be disingenuous so you've gotta be careful to not overshare information that could be used against you. Especially through messages where they can be screen captured and could get you in trouble.

On the flip side, Now I want you to use this power for good and not as insider information to manipulate your way up to corporate ladder, do what you will with your gift but karma does come around. And if you have ill intentions for being a good listener, it will come back to bite you someday. I am certain of it. People will know you are a faker and your reputation will precede you.

As you can clearly, being a good listener has immense pay offs for your personal and professional career. And learning to have an open ear could help you gain many potential friends at work and at play. How you respond when people share their stories and having a good character yourself personally also plays an important role in actually keeping these friends close to you as well, but being a good listener is a nice way to start.

I hope you learned something valuable today and I'll see you in the next one. Take care!

Chapter 5:
How To Deal With Feeling Anxious In A Relationship

There are different ways in which relationship anxiety can show up. A lot of people, when they are forming a commitment or when they are in the early stages of their relationship, feel a little insecure now; this is not something we would consider unusual, so if you have doubts or fears, you don't need to worry if they are not affecting you a lot. But sometimes, what happens is that these doubts and anxious thoughts creep into your day-to-day life. We will list some of the signs of relationship anxiety so you can figure them out for yourself, and then we will tell you how to deal with them.

1. Wondering if you matter to your partner
2. Worrying they want to breakup
3. Doubting your partners feeling for you
4. Sabotaging the relationship

These are some of the signs of relationship anxiety; now, it can take time to get to the roots of what is causing this. Right now, we will tell you how you can overcome it; yes, you read that right, you can overcome it no matter how hard it feels like at the moment. However, it will take time and consistent effort. The first thing you should do is manage anxiety early as soon as you see the symptoms because you keep delaying it. It will become a problem for you. What will help you is maintaining your identity. When you and your partner start getting closer, you will shift the key parts of your identity to make room for your partner and the relationship. You need to know that this does not help either of you. You will lose yourself, and your partner will lose the person they fell in love with. Secondly, practice good communication. If there is something specific they are doing that is fueling your anxiety, whether it's not making their bed after they wakeup or spending a lot of time on their phone, talk to them about it and try to be non-accusatory and respective about also use I statement these can be a huge help during such conversations. If you feel like things are getting out of control and you will not handle them on your own, talk to a therapist that will get you some clarity. Because it's a relationship issue, try talking to a therapist that works with couples because that can be particularly helpful for you, so if you both have any underlying needs, the therapist will be able to communicate that in a better way.

Chapter 6:
6 Signs You Need To Give Yourself Some Personal Space

While we wish to stay forever in the honeymoon phase of a relationship, we also must keep in mind that it is precisely what we call it; only a phase. Not every relationship is sunshine and rainbows every day. A relationship is between two individuals who both have individual needs. Sometimes, those needs include having some alone time with themselves. But how and when exactly do you know if you need some space from your partner?

April Masini, a New York-based relationship expert and author, says, "If you can't make it an hour or two without checking in or asking a question of your partner, you need a break." Needing space in your relationship does not in any way means that you don't love your partner anymore; it simply means that you need some time to get recharge and take care of yourself. Here are some signs that you need to give yourself some personal space.

1. **You Feel Stressed Out**

Suppose you're unnecessarily stressed out, even if it isn't coming from your relationship. In that case, it's probably a good idea to spend some alone time and ponder over things. It can be some underlying tension coming from work or family, or it might be something in your relationship that you want but are not necessarily getting it. Taking some time out for yourself and figuring out where your stress is coming from or what's been upsetting you, you will then be better positioned to sort out your problems and discuss those issues with your partner.

2. **You Don't Feel Like yourself**

A significant sign indicating that you need some alone time for yourself is if you are started to feel exhausted, irritable, or simply just not yourself. Everyone should know the importance of needing some me time for yourselves. Your partner should understand if you need to take care of yourself and your mental health. Needing space from your partner in no way means that your relationship is at stake or if there's anything wrong with it. It simply means that you both need to spend time with yourself to rest, relax, or spend time with other people.

3. **You Feel Suffocated**

Spending so much time with people can prove fatal and can lead to being co-dependent on them, which is ultimately the kiss of death. It is assumed that, as a couple, you both should naturally be spending all of your time together, but there is such a thing as seeing too much of each other. It is essential to pull away and have some time for yourself. Find a hobby, take a walk, read a book. The more you spend your time with a person, the more likely you will get tired of each other soon. You need to get yourself some personal space not to get suffocated and overwhelmed by your relationships with other people.

4. You Don't Have any Outside Interests

Do you have any interests of your own, or do you rely entirely on the other person and their hobbies? It's healthy to have some things in common with your partner, but not all of them. Suppose you follow and copy their hobbies and interests and don't have any of your own. In that case, it might lead to some adverse psychological effects. Suppose they leave you or are just too busy to see you; you'll be left with nothing but boredom and waiting for the other person to catch up to you again. You need to give yourself space and find out what you like as an individual. Find your hobbies and passions, grow fond of them, and then work on them independently.

5. Spending Time With Them Is Draining You Out

If you aren't having as much fun as you used to have while meeting them, then you should take some space for yourself. If you're feeling drained out and low on energy after every interaction, it's time to spend some time apart. You get frustrated and irritated easily and don't make any efforts to resolve a fight. Patch-ups seem challenging for you; if your interactions are painful and difficult, then consider some alone time to gather your thoughts.

6. Your Vibe's Getting A Bit Off

Although there can be many reasons for this, stress, depression, exhaustion, etc., the primary cause can be that you're not getting enough space to deal with your emotions and feelings. Your relationship feels strained, and you feel like escaping from everything. This is the best time to ask for space from everyone and everything and ponder over whatever's bothering you.

Conclusion

Everyone deserves a relationship with more positivity than negativity in it. It's okay to need some space for yourself now and then. Evaluate your needs and try to figure out what you want.

Chapter 7:
6 Ways To Deal With Arguments In A Relationship

Arguments are common in all kinds of relationships, be it with your parents, siblings, friends, or partner. Some degree of conflict can even be healthy as it shows that both of the partners are expressing themselves, rather than keeping their emotions fester and everything inside. Fighting consistently can also lead to a problematic relationship where you and your partner wouldn't be at peace. And if handled poorly, it can also become the cause of the downfall of your relationship.

It's normal to argue with your loved ones from time to time, but if the arguing is continuing at an unhealthy pace, or your disagreements are ending up in hostile silence, or worse, a screaming match, then it can take a severe toll on your life and affect it. Learning ways to handle disagreements constructively must be crucial in every relationship. Conflict is inevitable; it's how you deal with it that counts. Here are some of the ways to deal with arguments in a relationship.

1. **Find Out Why You're Arguing In The First Place**

Sometimes we look at the superficial layer of the issue, not the deeper layers that might discover the real reason behind the argument. If you and your partner frequently argue or about the same things, it can be good to evaluate what really is causing the conflict. You should see if the argument is really what you think you're arguing about, or are other factors involved too? Are there other things happening in your relationship that are worrying or frustrating you? You may want to consider other influences too, like, are there any significant changes happening in your life that's putting extra pressure on you? Maybe you're spending less time with your partner, and the cause of your arguments is sometimes unknown. Or perhaps you're both struggling with something that you aren't ready to talk about. Looking at the broader context of your situation and seeing past your emotions can be a great way to get to the bottom of what's going on.

2. **Talking It Over**

Talking calmly and constructively when you are actually overwhelmed and feeling emotional can be really difficult. It would be best if you gave yourself and your partner some time to cool off before starting the discussion again. It's essential to open up your feelings to your partner and ask them to do the same. If something's bothering you, you can always talk to your partner calmly and understandably rather than keeping it inside and only giving them hints. No one likes a guessing game in a relationship. Being vocal about your issues and hearing about your partner's, and then talking and sorting it out is critical.

3. **Try To Start The Discussion Amicably**

Don't start bypassing sarcastic or critical comments, mocking them, or aiming them with gun fires. It can only worsen the situation. Your partner may feel like you're insulting them and not respecting their emotions. Don't take the arguments personally and make it all about yourself. Try to be calm and patient and start by saying something positive like, "I feel like we have been arguing a lot lately; maybe we should discuss what's causing us both trouble and get back to our loving selves." This will not only make your partner feel important but also might end the argument all in all.

4. Try To See Things From Your Partner's Perspective

A conversation is likely to end up being productive if both partners aren't ready to listen to each other. It can be tempting to get your point across, but if you're looking to resolve things, you should take the time to hear about your partner's side too. They might have an entirely different perspective, but you need to understand it if you want to get to the root of what's causing you both to fight. Try to validate each other's feelings by hearing each other and comforting each other.

5. Keep Tabs On Physical Feelings

If the argument is getting too heated, take some time out to calm yourself and then continue once you're both feeling better. Don't pass remarks that you might later regret, or it could make your fight worse. It could end up leaving both of you seriously hurt.

6. Be Prepared to Compromise

Giving ground by both partners is often the only way to resolve a conflict. If both of you stick rigidly to your desired outcome, the fight would never come to an end. Sometimes, an imperfect solution can be better than having no solution at all. To move past things, one or both of the partners must compromise a little.

Conclusion

It can take some time and practice to disagree calmly and constructively and to change the negative behaviors. But if you stick with working together better, it can produce positive changes in your relationship. Forgive yourself and your partner and move on.

Chapter 8:
What To Do When You Have Thoughts of Breaking Up

It's not always easy deciding if you should break up with your partner: You probably care about them and have many great memories together. But there could be real issues in the relationship that make you wonder if it's best to end things. Whatever outcome you settle on, however, it's a good idea to first ask yourself a few questions so you can be sure it's the right decision for you.

"Breaking up with your partner is the best thing to do if you feel like you're not happy anymore, and the relationship is just pulling you down instead of pushing you up.
Here are some things to think about before ending your relationship, according to experts.

1. Is There Anyone Influencing My Decision?

If you're seriously considering breaking up with your partner, it's wise to take a moment to think about what — or, more specifically, who — might be influencing you toward this decision. Is your mom insisting you'd be better off without them? Does your best friend swear that splitting up is your best option? Although people's opinions can be a good guiding force, at the end of the day, this is your choice, not theirs.

2. Do We Hold the Same Core Values?

When you and your partner first got together, you might have initially bonded because you have similar interests. But if you're now at a place where you're thinking of taking the next steps or breaking up, it's worth asking yourself if the two of you align on values, too. "Preferences in daily life will change, but core values will likely not change. "You could feel like it is time to break up with your partner because those [incompatible] core values are showing themselves."

3. Would I Want My Child to Be With Someone Like My Partner?

It may seem like a strange thing to consider if starting a family isn't on the horizon, but it can be an effective litmus test to picture how you'd feel if your child were with someone like your partner. "This will trigger a reality check — would you want your children to spend the rest of their lives with the same kind of person as your partner? "If your answer is no, then take it as a sign that you are heading in the right direction ending the relationship."

4. Is This A Pattern for Me?

Are you someone who starts thinking of breaking up with your partner a few months in each time you're in a relationship? Do you start losing interest at about the one-year mark? Ask yourself whether this is a genuine impulse or if it's just a pattern for you. "Is the reason I desire to break up with someone unique to this person, or would it apply to multiple people?" Clara Artschwager, "If it applies to more than one person, this is often indicative of a larger limiting pattern in relationships."

Are you scared of getting too close to someone? Are you afraid of commitment? Reflecting on these things can help with your decision.

Chapter 9:
8 Signs That Someone Is Not Your Soulmate

When you find yourself in a relationship, everything feels fantastic. There are confused feelings everywhere, but those confusing feelings are just for the beginning. But we all do wonder if we'll ever find " the one." When we first enter a relationship, you may wonder if this is your soulmate. But sometimes, we want that one person to be our soulmate, but things just aren't meant to be that way. Here are a few signs that someone is not your soulmate.

1. **It is tough to trust them:**

If you feel yourself constantly spying about the whereabouts and motives of your partner because you feel like your partner is not honest with you, then you know that this person is not your soulmate. The reason behind this is that you can't just spend your whole life on the lookout. When you can't trust your soulmate no matter how much you try, you know that your partner is doing some shady stuff. A soulmate will be honest with their relationship even when you are not around because we all know, " Without trust, there is no relationship."

2. **You don't connect at an emotional level:**

In a relationship, you need to know all about your partner, about his life, his work, his future ambitions because if your connection with your partner is just surface level and you don't know anything about them, then you know that is not the "one." A soulmate would want to dig deeper into your soul and would want to know everything about you. Still, if you feel like they are not investing in the relationship and are not working for it, you may think that they are not interested in you or your life like a soulmate should be.

3. Your partner has different values than you:

Everyone has different values and meanings of life, but are these values too much further in your relationship? If so, then you know, this is not your soulmate. Indeed, a relationship requires compromise, but nobody can sacrifice too much, and having different values may as well result in that. Soulmates would have an essential, shared vision for the future.

4. He doesn't enhance your life:

A soulmate is someone who shows you a better side of yourself and life. A soulmate will make you feel complete, make you feel happy when you feel low, and give you the confidence you need. But if your partner makes no effort to help your personal growth or at least make you feel happy in your hard times, then you know that that is not your soulmate.

5. You wish to explore other interests:

It is entirely normal for a person that is in a relationship to find someone else attractive; after all, we all are human beings, but if you start picturing yourself with someone else and start wishing that you were single so you could explore other interests, then that is a huge sign you need to consider. When you find your soulmate, you would not wish to be single, and although other people still seem attractive, you would not want to leave your partner for them.

6. Your partner judges you:

All human beings have different views on life. Everybody thinks differently; indeed, there are things you and your partner do not have legal opinions on, and that is completely fine unless your partner starts judging you for doing something they don't like. Yes, a relationship does need compromise, but that surely does not mean that your partner gets the right to judge you because you did not compromise and still did something they don't like. A soulmate would never consider you for anything you do; a soulmate will understand you in the best possible way.

7. You don't feel the urge to text back:

Everybody knows that when you like someone, you reply to their messages as soon as you can. It is like a human being not to seem rude to the people they like, but if you don't want to reply to your partner, are you sure they are "the one"? If every other text you receive bothers you, and you don't feel that interested in them, you know that this person is not the one you were looking for.

8. **You don't just feel like telling him something important you:**

When you find the one, you want to tell them everything about yourself, including the essential things. But do you feel that way about your partner like you want to say everything about every day, or you just don't bother to tell? If you don't, then you know that he is not the one.

Conclusion:

Don't feel disheartened if you haven't found the right one yet because someone is made especially for you, and one day you will find your soulmate.

Chapter 10:
Make Time for Your Partner

When I first got into my relationship, I thought my boyfriend and my 100-hour workweek would have to battle it out until the bitter end. Yet somehow, I've managed to maintain both. It turns out there are a lot of weird [ways to make time for your partner](#) when you're busy AF. You may have to get creative and resort to some weird measures, but I am living proof that there is no such thing as being too busy for your loved ones.

We all have to run errands. That time is gone from your workday anyway. So, why not use it to show your partner you care instead of just getting what you need? Picking up each other's shampoo and favorite cereal (or, perhaps more practically, take turns picking up groceries and toiletries for the both of you) is one way to connect without needing to make any more time in your schedule.

You spend the same amount of time cooking for two people as you do for one, but since you're feeding two, you *save* time by doing this. Think about it: Instead of cooking every night, you only have to do it every *other* night. Even if you both eat it in front of your computers, making food for each other is a loving gesture that'll make you appreciate each other.

If you live together, you'll probably be sleeping in the same bed anyway. But even if you don't, your dates can consist solely of sleeping if that's what it takes to make time for each other. Or, if you can't sleep through the night with someone else next to you, you can try just sharing nap time.

Even if you don't get around to working out that much, the time you can devote to exercise will help clear your mind, so it's worthwhile if you can make it out for a short run or yoga class. Plus, [working out together can boost your attraction](#) by releasing endorphins.

I can't always handle this, especially when I need to feel like nobody wants my attention to focus. But for less intensive tasks, it can be comforting to cuddle up to your significant other while you're working. You can even be each other's sounding boards if you need help coming up with ideas.

This one will not work for everyone. But if you have an office in a similar place, your walk or ride to work can be your bonding time, even if it's just part of the way. Even just a shared walk to the train station can pay off if you think ahead enough to coordinate your trips to and from work.

Chapter 11:
7 Ways To Live Together In Harmony With Your Partner

A harmonious relationship can make a person's life happy and beautiful, but, unfortunately, not all of us are blessed with a harmonious relationship. It is essential to work on your relationship in order to make it work. Creating a harmonious bond between you and your partner can make your relationship more healthy and stable. The dream relationship of everybody is to feel loved, accepted, and respected but to achieve such a relationship, and you need to first work on yourself. You need to make sure that you are doing your best at making your partner feel loved.

Most people nowadays want to find their soulmates, but even when they see their soulmates, they don't have a peaceful relationship; the lack of harmony causes this.

Here are 7 ways to live together in harmony with your partner.

1. Accept Your Partners The Way They Are

The first step to a harmonious relationship is acceptance. It would be best to accept your partners the way they are; distancing them from yourself because of a simple mistake can lead to a toxic relationship. If you choose to love a person and be with them, you need to accept the good and bad in them. As they say that no one is perfect, we all are a work in progress. When you cannot receive your partner the way they are, a harmonious relationship cannot be achieved. It would help if you allowed them to evolve and support them throughout this journey.

2. Be Gentle And Compassionate

When you embody gentleness and compassion, your relationship bond deepens, and there is harmony in the relationship. Instead of jumping to conclusions and reacting dramatically, you need to respond with gentleness and understand your partner's feelings.

Compassion brings grace to a person. To achieve a harmonious relationship, you should give your partner grace to work on themselves, understand, and give them space to evolve and mature. It may take time, but it strengthens a relationship.

3. Expectations Should Be Released

With expectations comes disappointment. Expectations are the unspoken standards you expected your partner to live up to. When your partner does not live up to your expectations, you might feel upset or disappointed, but how can you have such high expectations from your partner about things that are unspoken. Work on letting go of these ideals that the society and your subconscious mind created about how a relationship should be. Release the attachment to situations turning out a specific way. Brace yourself for different outcomes of different situations. Don't expect too much from your partner because your partner, like you, cannot always live up to your expectation.

4. Personal Space In A Relationship

Every human being needs personal space; we often see couples that are always together. It may feel exciting and comforting at first, but everyone needs their personal space to think and function properly. After being with each other with no personal space, one can start feeling suffocated and may behave negatively. It would help if you had time to breathe, to expand, and to look within. To evolve, you need space. Personal space between couples proves that their relationship is healthy and robust.

5. Honesty

Honest communication is not just a factor to achieve a harmonious relationship but also to have any relationship at all. Not being truthful can cause conflicts and problems in a relationship. Moreover, being a liar can be a toxic trait that can cause your partner to end the relationship. But before being honest with your partner, you need to be honest with yourself. Know your true self, explore the good and bad in yourself. Don't hide your mistakes from your partner; instead, be honest and apologize to them before it is too late. Honesty is a crucial factor in achieving a harmonious relationship.

6. Shun Your Ego

Ego and harmony cannot simply go hand in hand; where ego exists, harmony cannot be established. Often by some people, ego is considered a toxic trait. This is the ego that stops a person from apologizing for his mistakes, which can create tension among the couple. The stubbornness to do things your way is caused by ego and can easily result in unwanted scenarios. These are not the components of a healthy relationship. So to establish a harmonious relationship, you should remove ego and learn to compromise a bit. By removing ego, you allow yourself to be more flexible and understanding.

7. Let Go if Unnecessary Emotional Pain

When you keep hurting over old resentments, you convert that pain into toxic feelings that are not good for a relationship. These poisonous feelings can make you make some bad decisions that may result in your partner feeling unsafe around you. This pain can cause you to bury your positives feeling inside. As a result of this, you may feel pessimistic and may exaggerate minor conflicts into something more. A person must let go of this emotional stress and pain. You can let go by going to a therapist or yoga and meditation. Once you have let go of the pain, your heart is now open to a peaceful and harmonious relationship.

To establish a harmonious relationship, you have to accept and understand your partner and work on yourself. Also, work on your radical integrity.

Chapter 12:

7 Ways To Deal With An Overly Jealous Partner

Being jealous in a relationship seems cute at first, but it can really kill the love you and your partner have for each other after a while. You'll probably start to see the negative aspects of over jealousy pretty clearly. Some people have bad experiences and trust issues due to their past relationships, so being in a relationship with a jealous person shouldn't necessarily be a deal-breaker. It can be started by finding why your partner is feeling the way they feel, especially when you haven't given them a reason to mistrust you in the first place.

If your partner is being aggressive and trying to control what you're doing, you might want to try to work together with them to fix the issue. It will give them the reassurance they need and create a closer bond between you two. If your partner is turning red with jealousy lately, here are some signs for you to deal with them.

1. **Talk About Their Fears and Anxieties**

It would be best to calmly sit your partner down with you and ask them what's going on in their mind if you feel like your partner's jealousy is getting off the hook. Make sure you're listening to them fully attentively, and don't be scared to express how their thoughts affect you. Danielle B.

Grossman, a California licensed marriage and family therapist, says, "Do not try to minimize, negate or 'fix' the fears. Do not try to bully your partner's fear into submission. Do not belittle, humiliate, shame, and threaten the fear." Always be empathetic and give them your undivided attention. Make sure you never attack your partner and make them trust that they can confide in you.

2. **Don't Get Defensive About Your Behavior**

If your partner is accusing you of something that is far from true, do not feed the fire by jumping right away into an argument. Evaluate the situation first. If you instantly try to get defensive, your partner will misinterpret your reaction or may get even angrier. Try to be patient first and deal with the situation calmly. Reassure them that whatever they're thinking isn't right, and you're always going to be with them no matter what.

3. **Be Extra Affectionate**

After discussing the reasons for their jealousy, show your partner extra love, during this weak and vulnerable time. This is the time to be more generous with your affection. Try to touch them more, make small gestures for them, and be supportive throughout this time. Of course, this means that you should take the abuse if extremely unhealthy jealousy is present. Don't let them force you into situations that you are uncomfortable dealing with.

4. **Create Boundaries**

Setting boundaries in your relationship isn't a negative thing at all. Loads of people in healthy relationships create a line to understand each other's emotions and priorities better. People should be aware of their selves even within a relationship. According to a Ph.D. psychologist Leslie Becker-Phelps, "You need to know what you like and dislike, what you're comfortable with versus what scares you, and how you want to be treated in the given situations." So, try your best not to let your mental health affect by your partner's conflicts.

5. **Be Available and Responsive:**

Although this issue is something that your partner needs to fix on their own, it can still help the situation get better if you're responsive when they reach out to you. If you're there when your partner needs you the most, and you tend to comfort them, it can help calm their jealous habits. This takes a lot of effort, without a doubt, but if your partner notices that you're available and receptive, then the trust between you two will only grow stronger with time.

6. **Revisit The Issue and Be Patient**

Over jealousy is an issue that can't be fixed overnight. You must be patient with your partner and show them now and then that you're willing to work on this problem together by supporting and discussing their fears. It can indeed be time-consuming and emotionally draining, but don't let it stop you from trying to work things out with your partner. Take baby steps, celebrate small victories until it isn't an issue anymore.

7. **Rebuild Your Trust**

If your partner is losing trust in you, make sure you gain it back by doing small things, such as facetiming them and texting them throughout the day, explaining to them why you're running late, or taking a rain check in advance if you know you're busy that day. Reassure them with positive statements, and this will eventually put your partner's fears at ease.

Conclusion

There's no magic spell or easy way to deal with a jealous partner, but if you want to make the relationship work, then put effort into it. Get your partner to trust you, be empathetic with them and talk about their feelings. This little bump in the road can probably go away, which will help you in the long run.

Chapter 13:
Learning To Trust Others

Today we're going to talk about a topic that has the potential to make or break your working relationships or personal relationships with others.

Trust is something that consistently ranks on the top of relationship goals and it has very good reasons for that. Without trust there is basically no foundation. When you can't trust someone, it basically means that you don't believe they can be left alone without your supervision. If you don't trust someone to do the work you have passed along to them, basically it means you are either micro-managing them all day long or that you might just end up doing the work entirely yourself because you don't believe that they can do a job up to your expectations. How many of you have experienced bosses who are micro-managers like that? Basically it either means that they think they can do a better job or that they don't trust you to do the work at all. And we all hate bosses who are like that. Look into mirror like that now, are you doing that to someone at your workplace now?

If you don't trust someone in a relationship, basically you don't believe that they can't be left to their own devices either if they are out of your sight. You start to worry about what they might do when you're gone. If a partner has cheated on you before, I bet that trust has probably gone out the window and it might take a lot of time and energy to actually start trusting that person again. If you don't trust a friend, you might not want to tell them secrets for fear that they may go round sharing it with others without your consent. That plays into the concept of trustworthiness as well. It all comes in a package.

To build trust, we have to earn it. With our actions we can show others that we can be trusted with information, secrets, work, to be faithful, and to do right thing at all times. But trust works both ways as well. If we want people to trust us, we must be willing to extend the trust to others as well. If others have displayed level of competency, we need to start learning to trust that they can get the work done without breathing down their necks all times of the day. If however they come back with shoddy work, maybe you might want to keep a closer eye on them before you feel that their work is up to your standards.

Let others prove to you otherwise by giving them the benefit of the doubt first and then assessing their abilities after.

When you show others that you trust them to do a task, more often than not they will feel a sense of urgency and responsibility to get the work done properly and promptly so that they can show you that they are capable. To show you that they are competent and worthy of the trust that you have placed in them. When you can learn to trust can you truly let go and live life freely. Always having to micro-manage others can not only hurt your reputation as "that guy" but also allow you to have more time do focus on areas where your attention is really required. When you can learn to trust can you truly expand and grow a team, business, company, friendships, and relationships.

I challenge each and everyone of you to learn to trust others and not feel like you have to manage everyone around you to the granular level. If you feel that you have trust issues, for whatever reason, consider working on it or maybe even seeking help. Trust issues usually stems from a past traumatic event or experience that may have impacted your ability to trust again. If so you may one to dig deeper to discover the root of the problem and work through it till the feeling goes away.

Take care and I'lll see you in the next one.

Chapter 14:
Dealing With Money in Relationships

When two people first get together, they don't know about each other's financial status. The way a person dresses can never tell how much money they have, as you might have seen people dress humbly but have quite a lot of money. On the other hand, some people spend their money on expensive items and clothes but, in reality, are not that rich. For many people, being financially stable is an essential factor in a relationship. As we have heard, many people say that when you love someone, truly money doesn't matter, but some people hold a different point of view.

However, it is entirely understandable that not everyone chooses love over money; for some people, money is a significant factor in life, but that doesn't mean that one should simply end things with their partner because of their low income. You can always encourage them and help them grow. Believing in your partner is an essential factor in every relationship; if your partner is trying to improve their financial status, then you should be there to give them the strength to continue their hard work.

One should always tell the truth about their income; lying will surely gain you some attention, but the person who truly loves you finds about your lie. It will be hard explaining it to them, and worse, it will end in an awkward situation. Money may attract attention, but in the end, the person who loves you will not be so happy with you, taking you for a lier they may end things. Hence, it is best always to be honest.

One should never date someone just because of their high income; you never know what that kind of person is like. Before starting a relationship, the best thing to do is to get to know each other because getting together with someone just because they are financially stable doesn't always end well. Getting together with someone just because of money can lead to a toxic relationship and may even turn into an abusive one. When you date someone for cash, your subconscious mind starts believing that your partner is the one in control, while in reality, both the partners have an equal role.

No one likes debt, but most of us have obligations. Sometimes, these debts are just a minor inconvenience, but other times, the burden is too much for a person to handle alone. So, always be honest about your financial situation, don't feel embarrassed; maybe when you share your case, your partner may also open about something. When you open up about your situation, you and your partner can find a solution together, and you can easily manage your debts and, with time, even get rid of them all.

When two people in a relationship decide to live together, it may be exciting at first, but the bills are always hard to pay. In such a case, you should always discuss these things with your partner about splitting the bill. Sometimes, you can't always divide the bill because your partner may not have told you but may be suffering from a few financial problems. So, it's better to discuss this kind of thing.

If things are coming to an end because of financial reasons, but you love each other and are willing to work it out, one should seek a relationship counselor. A relationship counselor is an expert at resolving such matters. The counselor can help resolve many problems, including debts, different spending habits, etc.

Always discuss your lifestyle choices if one of you has a costly taste, but your partner can't support it. That may become a problem; if such a problem occurs, then the best thing to do is to discuss such matters, as we all know a healthy relationship demands a person to compromise. Always remember that your relationship with this person is for a reason, so don't give up without trying, try to be honest, discuss things with your partner that is bothering you, and you would be well and good to go.

Chapter 15:

Feeling Insecure In Your Relationship

No matter how perfect a relationship sounds or seems, there is always something that pushes you off on the opposing side. That is feeling insecure. This feeling of being insecure is what makes us doubt ourselves and our partners. A relationship needs to build around trust and feeling secure in it. When you lack those factors, it's only natural that you might fall now or then; it often happens when you feel like your needs are not getting fulfilled by your partner. You will eventually come to realize that you wanted something else. It also occurs when you keep all the problems to yourself, thus, not trusting each other enough to share. These problems then become your demise, and eventually, you are unable to take them. You realize that going separate ways is the only option when you need a good conversation about your problems and listening to what your partner has to say. Giving them a chance and solving your problems together is how you will strengthen your bond, and that's how you will overcome your fears, as we all know that trust is the foundation of any relationship.

It would be best if you let go of things. When you start a relationship with a person you care about, you learn to leave something behind. You watch movies that they like or eat the food they want. Sacrifice is a common ground you both walk on. You have to learn to go by their choices sometimes. But, the same should be done with you. They should do the same for you, if not more. You both need to make some compensations along the way of your relationship. You have to give each other choices. You have to trust each other enough to know that they might be doing the right thing for you or making the right choice for you.

So, the most common factor is trust. Many relationships have been broken because of a lack of confidence. Trust comes very handily when you need to go through a difficult phase of your life. You need the support of your partner, and you just need them by your side. That means trusting them to stay with you through your worst. Growing together is what you need to fulfill in a relationship. And sometimes, while doing so, we meet disappointment. Lack of trust drives you to get annoyed quickly, and you start to get distant. Growing apart may seem complicated, but you think it's better than stay together. These insecurities are very hard to overcome, and all you would need is time. But, know that it is your mind speaking most of the time. That is why taking a chance is such a considerable risk that we sometimes do not bother with it. We have to game risk to know if there is a spark between you two to keep all the light alive. Or if it is just a dead end.

It would be best if you gave yourself a lecture on positivity now and then. It would help if you got rid of all the evil thoughts that are driving you towards doubt. Gain more confidence in yourself and gain more confidence in your partner. Believe in each other. Try to stay positive in every situation. And believe in the best possible outcome of your situation in your relationship. Surround yourself with good thoughts and feelings. Always motivate your partner in the best way possible and think of them as your equal. Share everything, good or bad, with them. You will see getting rid of your insecurities slowly by taking these small measures towards your relationship.

You just need to overcome your differences by talking and listening. Both of you need a little break now and then. You need to give them space often, but not such that they start to believe you are ignoring them. You need to shower your attention and make sure that this whole relationship works out in your favor. Don't get jealous of their interaction with another gender, but trust them to be loyal to you. Give them love and receive love from them. Insecurities are often built on false rumors or accusations. It would help if you stopped a little to process every time. And just know that in this case, your partner's words matter greatly. Make it work out, and try to feel as secure as possible with them around you.

Chapter 16:
What to Do When You Are At Different Life Stages In A Relationship

If you've started dating someone a lot older or younger than you and you haven't experienced any bumps along the way, it might be because your relationship is still relatively new.

"The issues begin, I think, to manifest themselves when people start to get into real-life situations. For example, if you don't want kids right away and you're dating someone who never wants them, it might not seem like an issue at the beginning. Still, later on, when you start to feel more ready to start a family, understandably, that tiny little thing can become a really big thing.

Not only that, but some people have had issues dating each other because they were at different stages in their lives. For example, while one might want to go out and dance with friends, the other might have no interest in spending time that way.

There are still ways to make a relationship work if you're at different stages in your life.

That doesn't necessarily mean that the relationship can't work just because you have different interests. For example, a woman said that her husband is ten years younger than her, and they don't have the same taste in music. But they each have friends to talk about those kinds of things, and it works for them.

"If you're dating someone with a big age difference, remember the reasons why you are drawn to that person," "Maybe you are very mature, and individuals your age aren't able to connect with you on a deeper level. Maybe you have a fun, energetic side, and you haven't been able to find a partner your age with similar interests and activities."

We advise that you do some reflection about what you want in the relationship to be clear on that and remind yourself of it when necessary.

Make sure your values, morals, and life goals match up.

"If you want the relationship to be long-term, then make sure that your values, morals, and life goals match.

Ask yourself a few specific questions before diving into something. Things like future goals, where you want to live, if you want a family, if you want religion to be part of your life, and if you see this person fitting in with your family and friends.

It's also important to consider what your relationship will look like down the line. "Big age differences aren't as noticeable when you're both middle-aged, but what happens once one of you is a senior, and the other isn't?" "These are the big picture questions that need to be thought about before you decide to spend your life together."

If you agree with each other on the big things, smaller things like having different tastes in music likely won't be as big of a deal. Just like in any relationship, you don't have to (and won't) agree on everything all the time. Although it might seem like you're farther apart on some topics than you would be if you're closer in age, other factors besides age might play a role in that.

Be prepared for others to comment on your relation.

There's a good chance that people will have opinions about your relationship." They'll ask questions, and they'll make comments that are probably pretty annoying, so be prepared with a response. Depending on who the person is, you might actually feel like you can get into an explanation of the relationship, but other times, it might not feel necessary, so just to be prepared with that,"

Ensure that the relationship's dynamic is equal and that one partner doesn't hold power over the other.

Each partner needs to avoid mothering the other, regardless of who's older or younger in the relationship. It can be difficult for those who take on that role, even among friends, to not act that way with their significant other, but she said that it's important to try to refrain. Sometimes mothering can turn into holding power over your partner, which isn't healthy behavior.

Chapter 17:
Don't Overthink Things

Analysis Paralysis, how many of you have heard of this term before? When a decision is placed before us, many of us try to weigh the pros and cons, over and over again, day and night, and never seem to be able to come up with an answer, not even one week later.

I have been guilty of doing such a thing many times in my life, in fact many in the past month alone. What I've come to realize is that there is never going to be a right decision, but that things always work out in the end as long as it is not a rash decision.

Giving careful thought to any big decision is definitely justified. From buying a car, to a house, to moving to another state or country for work, these are big life-changing decisions that could set the course for our professional and financial future for years to come. In these instances, it is okay to take as much time as we need to settle on the right calculated choice for us. Sometimes in these situations, we may not know the right answer as well but we take a leap of faith and hope for the best and that is the only thing we can do. And that is perfectly okay.

But if we translate the time and effort we take in those big projects into daily decisions such as where to go, what to eat, or who to call, we will find ourselves in a terrible predicament multiple times a day. If we overthink the simple things, life just becomes so much more complicated. We end up over-taxing our brain to the point where it does not have much juice left to do other things that are truly important.

The goal is to keep things simple by either limiting your choices or by simply going with your gut. Instead of weighing every single pro and con before making a decision, just go. The amount of time we waste calculating could be better spent into energy for other resources.

I have found that i rarely ever make a right choice even after debating hours on end whether I should go somewhere. Because i would always wonder what if i had gone to the other place instead. The human mind is very funny thing. We always seem to think the grass could be greener on the other side, and so we are never contented with what we have in front of us right here right now.

The next time you are faced with a non-life changing decision, simply flip a coin and just go with the one that the coin has chosen for you. Don't look back and flip the coin the other way unless it is truly what your heart wants. We will never be truly happy with every single choice we make. We can only make the most of it.

Chapter 18:
Dealing with Abuse in Relationship

Why can't they simply leave the relationship? This is one question that people frequently ask when they see someone is being abused in a relationship. But if you are the one who is in an abusive relationship, you will know that it not this easy. Ending a relationship that means a lot to you is never easy to end. It gets even more difficult when you have been psychologically beaten down, physically threatened, isolated from your friends and family, and financially controlled. If you are in an abusive relationship and want to leave, you might be feeling torn or confused—one moment you want to leave, the other you want to stay. You might even blame yourself for the abuse. If you are in an abusive relationship, we want you to remember;

- You are not to blame for being battered or mistreated.

- You deserve a safe and happy life.

- You are not the cause of your partner's abusive behavior.

- You are not alone. People are waiting to help.

- You deserve to be treated with respect.

- Your children deserve a safe and happy life.

Now, when you have to decide whether to stay in a relationship or to leave, here are some of the things you should keep in mind:

If you're hoping abusive partners will change, that is probably not going to happen; these people have deep psychological and emotional issues; although change is not something that is impossible but is not easy or quick, and change is only possible if the abuser takes full responsibility for their behavior.

Suppose you believe you can help your abuser. In that case, that is a natural phenomenon you will that you are the only one who understands them or that it is your responsibility to fix their problems. Still, the actual truth is that when you stay, you accept constant abuse, and you enable them, so instead of helping them, you are perpetuating the problem.

Suppose your partner has promised to stop the abuse. In that case, that is probably what they say at the moment because when they face, the consequences they plead for another chance and promise to change or beg for forgiveness. They might even mean it at the moment, but their actual goal is to stay in control and keep you from leaving them, and as soon as you will forgive them, they will return to their abusive behavior as soon as you forgive them because they are no longer worried that you will leave them.

Even If your partner is in counseling, there is no guarantee that they will change; there are many abusers that go through and continue to be violent, aggressive, controlling, and abusive. Suppose your partner has stopped making excuses and is showing visible signs of change, then that is good. However, you should decide based on who they are right now, not on the hope of who they would become.

If you are worried about what will happen once you leave, it is valid to be afraid of your abusive partner's will and where you will go, or how you will support your children or yourself. But you should not let this fear of the unknown keep you in an abusive relationship.

Here are some signs that your abuser is not changing

- They minimize the abuse or denies how serious it was.
- They pressurize you to make decisions about the relationship.
- They say that they can't change unless you stay with him and support him.
- You have to push him to stay in treatment.
- They tell you that you owe him another chance.
- They try to get sympathy from you, your children, or your family and friends.
- They claim that you're the abusive one.
- They pressure you to go to couple's counseling.
- They expect something from you in exchange for getting help.
- They continue to blame others for his behavior.

Chapter 19:
Being Authentic

Today we're going to talk about the topic of authenticity. This topic is important because for many of us, we are told to put on a poker face and to act in ways that are politically correct. We are told by our parents, Teachers, and many other figures of authority to try to change who we are to fit society's norms and standards. Over time this constant act of being told to be different can end up forcing us to be someone who we are not entirely.

We start to behave in ways that are not true to ourselves. We start to act and say things that might start to appear rehearsed and fake, and we might not even notice this change until we hear whispers from colleagues or friends of friends that tell us we appear to be a little fake. On some level it isn't our fault as well, or it might be. Whatever the reason is, what we can do however is to make the effort to be more authentic.

So why do we need to be authentic? Well technically there's no one real reason that clearly defines why this is important. It actually depends on what we want to expect from others and in life in general. If we want to develop close bonds and friendships, it requires us to be honest and to be real. Our friends can tell very easily when it seems we are trying to hide something or if we are not being genuine or deceptive in the things we say. If people manage to detect that we are insincerity, they might easily choose to not be our friend or may start to distance themselves from us. If we are okay with that, then i guess being authentic is not a priority in this area.

When we choose to be authentic, we are telling the world that we are not afraid to speak our mind, that we are not afraid to be vocal of our opinions and not put on a mask to try and hide and filter how we present ourselves. Being authentic also helps people trust you more easily. When you are real with others, they tend to be real with you too. And this helps move the partnership along more quickly. Of course if this could also be a quick way to get into conflicts if one doesn't practice abit of caution in the things that they say that might be hurtful.

Being authentic builds your reputation as someone who is relatable. As humans we respond incredibly well to people who come across as genuine, kind, and always ready to help you in times of need. The more you open up to someone, they can connect with you on a much deeper emotional connection.

If you find yourself struggling with building lasting friendships, stop trying to be someone who you are not. You are not Kim Kardashian, Justin Bieber, or someone else. You are you, and you are beautiful. If there are areas of yourself you feel are lacking, work on it. But make sure you never try to hide the real you from others. You will find that life is much easier when you stop putting on a mask and just embracing and being you are meant to be all along.

I challenge each and everyone of you to consider adding authenticity into everything that you do. Let me know the changes that you have experienced as a result of that. I hope you learned something today, thank you so much for being there and I'll see you in the next one.

Chapter 20:

7 Reasons Why Men Cheat

Men and women may cheat for different reasons, but it's likely due to the way men and women are socialized rather than any innate differences between them. The more we, as a society, move away from socialization and patriarchy, the less we see those gender differences in cheating behavior. However, nonetheless, research shows that men are more likely to cheat than women. The ratio is 20% of men have admitted to cheating compared to 13% of women.

We should never forget that our minds are more resilient than we give them credit for. Cheating in a relationship is solely that person's fault, no matter the circumstances. It can always be avoided if the person wants to. There are many reasons why men cheat, along with what defines cheating and signs to watch out for. Here are some reasons and behaviors that might apply to people of all genders but could be relevant to men.

1. **They're Looking For A Way Out**

Sometimes the first step for a man to get out of a relationship is to cheat. Although people of all genders might cheat, for this reason, men are most likely to do it. This is because men are less likely to have difficult conversations with their partners and seldom tell their own needs in a relationship. So, they see cheating as the only way out. Instead of having to bear the difficult conversation with their partner when they're done with their relationship, they escape through it all by the act of cheating and having an affair.

2. They're Looking For A Connection

Cheating doesn't always happen for physical reasons only, despite what gender norms might tell us about men. Feeling unseen, unheard, or disconnected from their partners can also contribute as a factor for it. Men are much less likely to have a sound social support system, and those things can hurt and make them go into a zone where they feel protected. In those instances, if a woman shows compassion and support, they welcome her with open arms. It might start with a friendship with someone who will make him feel better about himself, and hence, an emotional connection forms.

3. They Have Sociopathic or Narcissistic Traits

If a partner has cheated, there could be more than just finding a way out of their relationship. There can be narcissistic tendencies or sociopathic traits involved. They could be someone who doesn't care about their partner's feelings, and they might do it simply because they want to. When an opportunity to cheat presents itself, they go towards it without giving a damn about their partner.

4. Revenge Cheating

Some people act on their impulses and cheat out of anger, jealousy, or desire revenge. It's not necessary that their partner might have cheated on them; even if they have done something slight to upset them (like having a close friendship with another man), they'll end up cheating on their partner to make a point.

5. Struggles With Substance Abuse

Cheating becomes more likely if one is dealing with a substance abuse problem. Substance addiction can create an impulse-driven and more immature version of ourselves. Many relationships tend to fall apart if one of the two partners has become addicted to a substance and acts subconsciously on their impulse.

6. They Seek Validation

If someone is not getting validation in their relationship, then insecurity and low self-esteem can drive them to cheat. If they don't feel attracted enough to their partner, they may cheat to seek external validation. Sexual issues can also cause someone to look for someone newer to prove themselves to.

7. They're Emotionally Immature

Emotional immaturity is sometimes the core of why men cheat. Since childhood, men are expected and taught not to talk about their feelings and emotions. This inability to speak leads to several issues and conflicts in their relationships. By the time you know it, they are having an affair and cheating on their significant other. Cheating can be an essential consequence of poor judgment, lack of willpower, self-control, and immaturity. A mature man will always talk about his feelings and resolve conflicts and issues with his partner.

Conclusion:

Being cheated on can be the worst trauma anyone can experience, and there can be so many reasons it might have happened in different relationships and contexts. But no matter the reason, it cannot be denied that infidelity forces both of you to step back. Analyze what went wrong and decide how you both want to move forward from there.

Chapter 21:
What Happens When You Get Bored In A Relationship

Being bored in your relationship can make you feel unpleasant emotions; you would not feel like yourself. You will be more likely to be over things that excited you before, like sex, date night, vacation with your partner, etc. Even if you don't feel like ending things, the lack of satisfaction would be enough to get you frustrated and ready to break up. Due to this boredom, you may feel stuck in a tedious cycle or feel suffocated. There are many things you will notice about yourself when you are bored of your relationship.

Picking unnecessary fights with your partner is one of the signs that you are bored with them. Dr. Binita Amin, a clinical psychologist, says getting into arguments for innocuous reasons might signify you are bored. If you find yourself bickering with your partner for petty reasons, then you may want to step back and assess why. Boredom can efficiently fuel arguments, but disagreements happen in any relationship; the best way is to see if these arguments are indeed caused by boredom.

Your frustration with your relationship causes these arguments. You can always figure out what is exactly causing this boredom, and maybe you can overcome this problem and carry out a healthy relationship.

Sometimes, we all enjoy comfortable silence, but is that silence comfortable anymore, or is it just because you have no more to speak to each other. Silent meals even when you are in a sit-in restaurant, or even if a few words are exchanged, but those words are in safe and predictable confines, then that is a sign that you are bored. To prevent this, you can try strengthening your bond with your partner.

When we first meet a person we like or at the beginning of a relationship, we put our best self forward, we try to be perfect for them, but when a person feels bored, they no longer place any effort into their relationship. They don't bother looking nice for a date night or don't bother waiting for them at the dinner table because we all know such factors lead to a healthy relationship. Being bored in a relationship can lead to an unhealthy period of your life. But if you are putting in the effort, you know that boredom is far away from your relationship and you.

Have you ever wondered about what it would be like to be with someone else? Even when you are in a relationship. If you have, then that is a sign that you have fallen victim to boredom. It is natural for a person to find more than one person attractive but always pay attention to what is the factor that is causing you to daydream about someone else, and it is simply because you are bored with your relationship. Because if that is the case, you need to make your relationship more exciting or talk and discuss matters with your partner.

Many people in this world are happy to be single, as they say, to be free of any commitment but are that the case with you. Do you wish that you were single? Or envying the single status of your friends? If yes, then you need to take a closer look at your relationship; it may turn out that you feel bored with your relationship, that you no longer feel the passion and excitement of the earlier days of your relationship. If you are glad that your partner is busy with something else, then that is a sign that you are bored.

Don't let boredom be the end of your relationship; you can seek help from relationship counselors, or you can sit around and discuss these matters. Together you can always find a solution to every problem. All relationship requires efforts, so put in your step and let your relationship bloom.
.

Chapter 22:

<u>6 Ways to Stay Committed in a Relationship</u>

Intro:

Once you and your partner decide to transition from a newly dating into a long-term committed relationship, you will experience some challenges and changes. A long term relationship will come with a lot of benefits. You will be closer to each other and also more comfortable in each other's presence. But it will also come with some difficulties, you will have to put in work, but you do not have to complicate it. You should focus on establishing healthy standards and habits that work for both of you. We are going to list 6 ways that will help you stay in a committed relationship.

1. **Communication:**

Now, this might not sound like a piece of revolutionary advice, but communication is a critical factor for a healthy, committed relationship. When your communication is based on honesty, the trust in your relationship will increase, and your partner will also feel supported and safe if you are prone to people-pleasing than deep, real, effective communication can be exhausting. But you can only have a healthy relationship if you voice your opinions and tell them what is bothering you. Good communication also means recognizing all the things you are grateful for in the relationship. After all, healthy communication is not always negative.

2. Engage in Self-Growth:

It is essential to focus on personal goals and self-growth even when you are in a relationship. Most people fall into the trap of investing most of their energy in the relationship and their partner, and they forget to prioritize their own needs and wants, which results in them feeling exhausted most of the time. To make a relationship healthy, it is essential to recognize your needs and then voice them. When you focus on actualizing your goals and self-care, you will feel more fulfilled, which will lead to you feeling more comfortable in your relationship.

3. Boundaries:

An essential part of relationships is boundaries. They can be emotional, sexual or physical. You need to set and communicate your boundaries with your partner in a committed relationship. When you have been together for a very long time, your partner might assume that some things are fine with you when in reality, they are not. At the beginning of the relationship, you let things slide because perhaps you did not have the confidence to talk about them or maybe your views on certain things have changed. Regardless it is important to set healthy boundaries so your relationship can flourish.

4. Focus on Intimacy:

Intimacy is much more than your sex life. The intimacy that will foster trust between you and your partner is physical and emotional closeness. Often when people are in long-term relationships, they forget the importance of intimacy. When you get comfortable around your partner, often you forget to show your love and affection. You might think it is silly of you to keep saying I love you over and over again. You have been together for a long time, and of course, they know it, but that is not the case; to have a healthy relationship, you need to remind your partner that you still care and matter to you.

5. Appreciate Your Differences:

You and your partner are two unique individuals with different perspectives, pasts, and destinations. You need to recognize this. Maybe these differences are what make you such a great couple. Even if you are not the opposite attracts kind of couple, you will have some differences that are the reason for friction in your relationship. You should never try to change your partner, whether there are some larger things you think need to change or small things that irritate you. You should accept them for who they are, with their differences for a healthy relationship.

6. Relish:

There can be times when your relationship goes awry, and you will need professional help to get back on track, and even if that is not the case, there can be times when you are just looking for advice to improve your relationship and make it more healthy. If you have found yourself in the same situation, you should consider downloading an app called "Relish". Relish is an app designed for relationship coaching. It can help you and your partner evaluate the current status of your relationship and help identify how you can improve your relationship. Professional coaches are available on relish, which can help you with different relationship struggles you are facing and put your relationship back on a healthy track.

Conclusion:

You need to have a healthy, long-lasting relationship, and we are sure these 6 ways will go a long way. With time a relationship can turn toxic, and there is no big deal in that you just have to know how you can fix that. Lastly, you should never forget about your personal growth and priorities and goals because that will satisfy you.

Chapter 23:
Being 100% Happy Is Overrated

Lately I've been feeling as though happiness isn't something that truly lasts. Happiness isn't something that will stay with us very long. We may feel happy when we are hanging out with friends, but that feeling will eventually end once we part for the day. I've been feeling as though expecting to be constantly happy is very overrated. We try to chase this idea of being happy. We chase the material possessions, we chase the fancy cars, house, and whatever other stuff that we think will make us happy. But more often than not the desire is never really fulfilled. Instead, i believe that the feeling accomplishment is a much better state of mind to work towards. Things will never make us happy. We may enjoy the product we have worked so hard for temporarily. But that feeling soon goes away. And we are left wondering what is the next best thing we can aim our sights on. This never-ending chase becomes a repetitive cycle, one that we never truly are aware of but constantly desire. We fall into the trap that finding happiness is the end all-be-all.

What i've come to realise is that most of the time, we are actually operating on a more baseline level. A state that is skewed more towards the neutral end. Neither truly happy, or neither truly sad. And I believe that is perfectly okay. We should allow ourselves to embrace and accept the fact that it is okay to be just fine. Just neutral. Sure it isn't something very exciting, but we shouldn't put ourselves in a place where we expect to be constantly happy in order to lead a successful life. This revelation came when I realised that every time I felt happy, I would experience a crash in mood the next day. I would start looking at instagram, checking up on my friends, comparing their days, and thinking that they are leading a happier life than I was. I would then start berating myself and find ways to re-create those happy moments just for the sake of it. Just because I thought i needed to feel happy all the time. It was only when I actually sat down and started looking inwards did I realise that maybe I can never truly find happiness from external sources.

Instead of trying to find happiness in things and external factors that are beyond my control, I started looking for happiness from within myself. I began to appreciate how happy I was simply being alone. Being by myself. Not letting other factors pull me down. I found that I was actually happiest when I was taking a long shower, listening to my own thoughts. No music playing, no talking to people, just me typing away on my computer, writing down all the feelings I am feeling, all the thoughts that I am thinking, letting every emotion I was feeling out of my system. I started to realise that the lack of distractions, noise, comparisons with others, free from social media, actually provided me with a clearer mind. It was in those brief moments where I found myself to be my most productive, with ideas streaming all over the place. It was in that state of mind that I did feel somewhat happy. That I could create that state of mind without depending on other people to fulfil it for me.

If any of you out there feel that your emotions are all over the place, maybe it is time for you to sit down by yourself for a little while. Stop searching for happiness in things and stuff, and sometimes even people. We think it is another person's job to make us happy. We expect to receive compliments, flowers, a kiss, in order to feel happy. While those things are certainly nice to have, being able to find happiness from within is much better. By sitting and reflecting in a quiet space, free from any noise and distractions, we may soon realise that maybe we are okay being just okay. Maybe we don't need expensive jewellery or handbags or fancy houses to make us happy. Maybe we just need a quiet mind and a grateful spirit.

The goal is to find inner peace. To accept life for the way it is. To accept things as the way they are. To be grateful for the things we have. That is what it means to be happy.

Chapter 24:

6 Signs Your Love Is One Sided

While some things are better one-sided, like your favorite ice-cream cone that you don't want to share, your high school diary that knows all your enemies and crushes, and a game of solitaire. But a healthy relationship? Now that should be a two-sided situation. Unfortunately, when you're stuck in a one-sided relationship, it becomes easy to fool yourself every day that what you are experiencing is normal, when in reality, it could actually be toxic or even unworthy and loveless.

They could physically be sitting next to you, but you will find yourself being alone because of your emotional needs not being taken care of. Even though you have committed yourself to your partner, there's a fundamental difference between being selfless in love and giving it all without receiving anything at all. It might be possible that you're in denial, but the below signs of your one-sided love are hard to ignore.

1. You're Constantly Second-Guessing Yourself

If you don't get enough reassurance from your partner and constantly wonder if you are pretty enough, or intelligent enough, or funny enough, and always trying to live up to your partner's expectations, then you're definitely in a one-sided relationship. You tend to focus all of your energy and attention on being liked instead of being your true self and nurtured by your partner. It would be best if you always were your authentic self so the people who genuinely deserve you can get attracted to you and get relationships that match the true you.

2. You Apologize More Than Needed

Everyone makes mistakes. We are not some divine creatures who are all perfect and have no flaws. Sometimes you're at fault, sometimes your partner is. But if you end up saying sorry every single time, even if you had no idea about the fight, then maybe take a deeper look at your relationship. You may think that you're saving your relationship by doing this, but trust me, this is a very unhealthy sign. Cori Dixon-Fyle, founder and psychotherapist at Thriving Path, says, "Avoiding conflict results in dismissing your feelings." Solving fights should always be a team approach and not just one person's responsibility.

3. You're Always Making Excuses For Your Partner

Playing defense is excellent, but only on a soccer team. Suppose you are doing it constantly for your partner and justifying their behaviors to your circle of friends, family, and work colleagues. In that case, you're overlooking something that they are most likely seeing. If the people in your life are constantly alarming you, then maybe you should focus on your partner and see where the signs are coming from.

4. You Feel Insecure About Your Relationship

If you are never indeed at ease with your partner and often question the status of your relationship, then it's a clear sign that you are in a one-sided relationship. If you focus more on analyzing yourself, becoming more alluring, and choosing words or outfits that will keep your partner desiring you, then it's a major red flag. To feel unsettled and all-consumed in a relationship is not only exhausting, but it's also sustainable. Feeling constantly depleted in your relationship is also a sign that it's one-sided.

5. You're Giving Too Much

Giving too much and expecting just a little can never work in the long run. Suppose you're the only one in the relationship who makes all the plans. Do all the chores, remember all the important dates and events, consider stopping or making your partner realize that they aren't giving much in the relationship. Often when people give, they have some expectations in the back of their mind that the giving will be returned, but things fall apart when the other person never had those intentions. It's normal for a short while for one partner to carry the load more than the other; all relationships go through such stages, but constantly engaging in it is unhealthy.

6. You're Never Sure About How They Are Feeling

You can't read people's minds, nor are the communications transparent; you may end up overthinking their behaviors towards you and may be confused about how they're truly feeling. This uncertainty would cause you to dismiss your feelings in favor of thinking about them. This connection may be filled with guessing and speculations rather than knowing reality and seeing where they genuinely stand.

Conclusion

The best way to fix a one-sided relationship is to step away and focus on your self-worth and self-growth instead of trying to water a dead plant. You must focus on flourishing your own life instead of shifting your all to your partner. Your mental health should be your priority.

Chapter 25:
How To Worry Less

How many of you worry about little things that affect the way you go about your day? That when you're out with your friends having a good time or just carrying out your daily activities, when out of nowhere a sudden burst of sadness enters your heart and mind and immediately you start to think about the worries and troubles you are facing. It is like you're fighting to stay positive and just enjoy your day but your mind just won't let you. It becomes a tug of war or a battle to see who wins?

How many of you also lose sleep because your mind starts racing at bedtime and you're flooded with sad feelings of uncertainty, despair, worthlessness or other negative emotions that when you wake up, that feeling of dread immediately overwhelms you and you just feel like life is too difficult and you just dont want to get out of bed.

Well If you have felt those things or are feeling those things right now, I want to tell you you're not alone. Because I too struggle with those feelings or emotions on a regular basis.

At the time of writing this, I was faced with many uncertainties in life. My business had just ran into some problems, my stocks weren't doing well, I had lost money, my bank account was telling me I wasn't good enough, but most importantly, i had lost confidence. I had lost the ability to face each day with confidence that things will get better. I felt that i was worthless and that bad things will always happen to me. I kept seeing the negative side of things and it took a great deal of emotional toll on me. It wasn't like i chose to think and feel these things, but they just came into my mind whenever they liked. It was like a parasite feeding off my negative energy and thriving on it, and weakening me at the same time.

Now your struggles may be different. You may have a totally different set of circumstances and struggles that you're facing, but the underlying issue is the same. We all go through times of despair, worry, frustration, and uncertainty. And it's totally normal and we shouldn't feel ashamed of it but to accept that it is a part of life and part of our reality.

But there are things we can do to minimise these worries and to shift to a healthier thought pattern that increases our ability to fight off these negative emotions.

I want to give you 5 actionable steps that you can take to worry less and be happier. And these steps are interlinked that can be carried out in fluid succession for the greatest benefit to you. But of course you can choose whichever ones speaks the most to you and it is more important that you are able to practice any one of these steps consistently rather than doing all 5 of them haphazardly. But I want to make sure I give you all the tools so that you can make the best decisions for yourself.

Try this with me right now as I go through these 5 steps and experience the benefit for yourself instead of waiting until something bad happens.

The very first step is simple. Just breathe. When a terrible feeling of sadness rushes into your body out of nowhere, take that as a cue to close your eyes, stop whatever you are doing, and take 5 deep breaths through your nose. Breathing into your chest and diaphragm. Deep breathing has the physiological benefit of calming your nerves and releasing tension in the body and it is a quick way to block out your negative thoughts. Pause the video if you need to do practice your deep breathing before we move on.

And as you deep breathe, begin the second step. Which is to practice gratefulness. Be grateful for what you already have instead of what you think u need to have to be happy. You could be grateful for your dog, your family, your friends, and whatever means the most to you. And if you cannot think of anything to be grateful for, just be grateful that you are even alive and walking on this earth today because that is special and amazing in its own right.

Next is to practice love and kindness to yourself. You are too special and too important to be so cruel to yourself. You deserve to be loved and you owe it to yourself to be kind and forgiving. Life is tough as it is, don't make it harder. If you don't believe in yourself, I believe in you and I believe in your worthiness as a person that you have a lot left to give.

The fourth step is to Live Everyday as if it were your last. Ask yourself, will you still want to spend your time worrying about things out of your control if it was your last day on earth? Will you be able to forgive yourself if you spent 23 out of the last 24 hours of your life worrying? Or will you choose to make the most out of the day by doing things that are meaningful and to practice love to your family, friends, and yourself?

Finally, I just want you to believe in yourself and Have hope that whatever actions you are taking now will bear fruition in the future. That they will not be in vain. That at the end of the day, you have done everything to the very best of your ability and you will have no regrets and you have left no stone unturned.

How do you feel now? Do you feel that it has helped at least a little or even a lot in shaping how you view things now? That you can shift your perspective and focus on the positives instead of the worries?

If it has worked for you today, I want to challenge you to consistently practice as many of these 5 steps throughout your daily lives every single day. When you feel a deep sadness coming over you, come back to this video if you need guidance, or practice these steps if you remember them on your own.

I wish you only good things and I hope that I have helped you that much more today. Thank you for your supporting me and this channel and if you find that I can do more for you, do subscribe to my channel and I'll see you in the next one. Take care.

Chapter 26:
Don't Make Life Harder Than It Needs To Be

Today we're going to talk about a topic that I hope will inspire you to make better decisions and to take things more lightly. As we go through this journey of life together, and as we get older, we soon find ourselves with more challenges that we need to face, more problems that we need to solve, and more responsibilities that we need to take on as an adult. In each phase of life, the bar gets set higher for us. When we are young, our troubles mostly revolve around school and education. For most of us we don't have to worry much about making money or trying to provide for a family, although I know that some of you who come from lesser well off families might have had to start doing a lot earlier. And to you i commend you greatly. For the rest of us we deal with problems with early teenage dating, body image, puberty, grades, and so on. It is only until we graduate from university do we face the harsh reality of the real world. Of being a working adult. It is only then are we really forced to grow up. To face nasty colleagues, bosses, customers, you name it. And that is only just the beginning.

Life starts to get more complicated for many of us when we start to realise that we have to manage our own finances now. When our parents stop giving us money and that we only have ourselves to rely on to survive. Suddenly reality hits us like a truck. We realise that making our own money becomes our primary focus and that we may not have much else to rely on. We take on loans, mortgages, credit card debts, and it seems to never really end. For many of us, we may end up in a rat race that we can't get out of because of the payments and loans that we have already ended up committing to. The things we buy have a direct impact on the obligations that have to maintain.

Next we have to worry about finding a partner, marriage, starting a family, buying a house, providing for your kids, setting aside money for their growth, college fund, the list goes on and on.

Do you feel overwhelmed with this summary of the first maybe one-third of your life? The reality is that that is probably the exact time line that most of us will eventually go through. The next phase of life requires us to keep up the payments, to go to our jobs, to keep making that dough to sustain our family. We may have to also make enough money to pay for tuition fees, holidays, gifts, payments to parents, and whatever other commitments that we might have. And this might go on until we reach 60, when two-thirds of our lives are already behind us.

Life as you can see, without any external help, is already complicated enough. If you didn't already know by now, life isn't easy. Life is full of challenges, obligations, obstacles, commitments, and this is without any unforeseen events that might happen... Medical or family wise.

With all this in mind, why do we want to make life harder than it already is?

Every additional decision that you make on top of this list will only add to your burden, if it is not the right one, and every person that you add into your life that is negative will only bring the experience much less enjoyable.

To make life easier for you and your soul, I recommend that you choose each step wisely. Choose carefully the partner that you intend to spend your life with, choose wisely the people that you choose to spend your time with, choose wisely the food that you put in your body, and choose wisely the life that you wish to lead.

Be absolutely clear on the vision that you have for your life because it ain't easy.

Another thing to make your life much less complicated is to put less pressure on yourself. I believe that you don't need to start comparing your life with others because everyone is on their own journey. Don't chase the fancy houses and cars that your friends have just because they have them. Everyone is different and everyone's priorities might be different as well. They might pride having a luxury car over spending on other areas of life, which might differ from the interests that you might have. Comparison will only most certainly lead you to chase a life that you might not even want to attain. And you might lose your sleep and mind trying to match up to your peers. Focus on yourself instead and on exactly what you want out of life and it will definitely be enough.

I challenge each and everyone of you to have a clear set of priorities for yourself. And once you have done so and are working towards those goals, be contented about it. Don't change the goalpost just because your friends say you must, or because you are jealous of what they have. Be satisfied in your own path and life will reward you with happiness as well.

I hope you learned something today. Thank you and I'll see you in the next one.

Chapter 27:
10 Thoughts That Can Destroy Relationships

You might enjoy the beauty and joy that comes with being in a loving and committed relationship, but it's not always butterflies and beds of roses. It's ubiquitous for you or your partner to transform your insecurities into fears and negative thoughts, but they don't treat you right; they may take a toll on your relationship. Negative thoughts may turn into negative actions, which can lead to unhealthy communication, and could impact how you start seeing your significant other. If you relate to any of the below thoughts, it might be time to reevaluate your relationship and how you view the situation.

1. **They don't love me anymore:**

Although it's pretty common to worry about whether the sparks of love are still alive in your partner's heart or not, constantly asking them whether they still love you might do more harm than good. It could stir up a lot of conflicts based on your insecurities and fears. Even if your partner reassures you by saying that they love you, it could put them in doubt as to there must be a matter causing these concerns. Instead of swinging and jumping to conclusions, communicate effectively with your partner in a way that's suitable for both of you.

2. **The power word "should":**

It is more or less a major red flag to not tell your partner about what you're thinking rather than automatically assuming that they should know how to read your mind. Blaming your partner for understanding the things that are affecting you secretly, like, "he should know how much it bothers me when he doesn't give me time" or "she should understand how busy i am these days" isn't fair at all. You should be able to voice all your frustrations but in a way that you make your partner understand and not push them away.

3. **The blame game:**

It's easier to point fingers at your partner and blame them for your spoiled mood rather than taking actions against yourself. Blaming them only postpones any improvements that are needed in your relationship. Instead, try talking to them about it. Tell them when they are wrong and apologize for something that you did to hurt them. We can never predict or control others' emotions, but we can very well hold our own.

4. **Overactive imagination:**

This mostly happens when you're overthinking about a situation and jump straight to conclusions without having any actual evidence. For instance, if your partner is coming home late at night and they're telling you it's because of the heavy workload, you automatically assume it's because they're having an affair and they're lying to you. These may happen when you have a piece of unattended emotional baggage from previous relationships. It's important to understand that you know your partner well, and they will never do such a thing to hurt you. Have a conversation with your partner about this and seek reassurance if needed.

5. **Comparing and contrasting:**

You start to put your partner under the pressure of unrealistic expectations when you compare them with a person you see as ideal. For example, if you met your best friend's boyfriend and witnessed an action they did, and you wished that your boyfriend should do the same, you might be disrespecting your partner by asking them to change into who they aren't. It's unhealthy to put that sort of pressure on them. Instead, ask your partner politely if they're willing to do that for you since you liked a particular quality or trait in a person, but you should also tell them that they are lovable regardless.

6. **Fantasizing:**

Unless you are in a toxic relationship, reminiscing and fantasizing about someone other than your partner might badly affect your relationship. It's because you will keep thinking about the possibilities of being with someone else rather than working on the flaws of your relationship. This might destroy your relationship in ways you can't even imagine.

7. **All or nothing:**

Seeing your partner as a perfect human being without mistakes, flaws, or imperfections is an idea for destruction. Having extreme thoughts that they can do no wrong or thinking that they always do the wrong thing can mess up with your own and your partner's mental health. Try accepting their failures and mistakes, and keep in mind that, like you, they're just ordinary human beings.

8. **Label slinging:**

Constantly putting labels on your partner, like calling them lazy when they couldn't complete their chores or calling them insensitive if they don't address a particular issue, may cause problems in your relationship. Instead, we should try to see the positive things in them and help them improve themselves.

9. **You think you can't compete with their ex:**

Their ex is their ex for a reason. Constantly trying to be like them and asking about them isn't helpful in any way; it can make your relationship weak and your partner frustrated.

10. **You think that you're hard to love:**

Worrying about pushing your partner away while addressing your insecurities is normal, but that doesn't in any way mean that you're hard to love. Everyone is special and unique in their tracks and can be loved by their partner no matter what.

Conclusion:

While these thoughts might be the perfect recipe to destroy your relationship, a little effort, and hard work into it can go a long way and save your relationship.

Chapter 28:
7 Ways To Attract Happiness

We have seen a lot of people defining success as to their best of knowledge. While happiness is subjective from person to person, there's a law of attraction that remains constant for everyone in the world. It states that you will indirectly start to attract all the good things in life when you become happier. This is why happy people often have good lives where everything just somehow tends to work for them. Happiness not only feels good but can also make our manifestation attempts twice as effective. We shouldn't measure our happiness from external factors but instead, as cliche as it may sound, we should know that true happiness comes from the inside.

Here are some ways for you to attract happiness:

1. **Make a choice to be happy:**

When you choose to be as happy as you can in every moment of your life, your subconscious mind will start acknowledging your decision, and it will begin to find ways to bring more joy into your life. When you work towards your decision of being happy, the universe also plays its part and makes sure it attracts more situations in your life that you can be pleased about. The positive vibrations that you will give out will find their way back to you. You don't have to make the decision of being happy right away, as some of you might be going through a tough time. Sit, relax, and take some time to reflect on yourself first and then make a choice whenever you're ready.

2. Define What Happiness Means To You

We have also found ourselves asking this question a million times, "what exactly is happiness?" Some people would attach the idea of happiness with materialistic things such as a big house, expensive cars, branded clothes and shoes, designer bags, the latest technologies, and so forth. While for some, happiness is merely spending time with family and friends, doing the things that they love, and finding inner peace and calm.

3. React Positively under all situations:

We could experience a thousand good things but a million bad ones in our everyday lives. And sometimes, it could be complicated for us to encounter any kind of happiness given the circumstances. Although these circumstances cannot be in our control, how we react to them is always in our hands. As our favorite Professor Dumbledore once said, "Happiness can be found even in the darkest of times if only one remembers to turn on the light." Similarly, we should always try to find that silver lining at the end of the dark tunnel, always seek some positivity in every situation. But we are only humans. Don't try to enforce positivity on yourself if you don't feel like it. It's okay to address all our emotions equally till you be yourself again.

4. Do not procrastinate:

You might find it a bit weird, but procrastination does snatch your happiness away. No matter how much things are going well in your life, you would always find a loophole, a reason to be unhappy and dissatisfy with yourself a well as your life. Procrastination makes you believe that you are not living up to your fullest potential. You will get this nagging feeling that will eventually morph into negative emotions that would nearly eat you. So, try to avoid procrastination as much as possible and start doing the things that actually matter.

5. **Stay present:**

The key to becoming more focused, more at peace, more effective in manifesting, and eventually, much happier is to just live in the moment. Whatever you're doing in the present, try to be completely aware and focused on it. It will help you avoid all the negative feelings you have conjured up about the past and future. Try to stay present as much as you can; over time, it will become a habit, and you will develop the capability to face it all. This will definitely help you attract more happiness into your life.

6. **Do not compare yourself:**

As Theodore Rosevelt once said, "Comparison is the thief of joy." Whenever we compare ourselves to others, we tend to become ungrateful and strip ourselves of the ability to appreciate the good and abundance in our lives. We start to magnify the good in other people's lives and the bad that is in our own. We must understand that everyone is going through their own pace, and they all are secretly struggling with one thing or the other.

7. Don't try too hard:

Happiness demands patience. It is better to get into it gradually rather than being overeager. Many people take the law of attraction and being positive a little too far and start obsessing over it. They tend to panic if they get negative thoughts or are unable to attract the things they want. Don't get frustrated if things don't work out your way, and don't give up on the idea of happiness if you feel distressed. Try to prioritize your happiness and give others a reason to be happy too. Make yours as well as other's lives easy.

Conclusion:

Not many people know that, but being happy is actually the foundation towards attracting all your dreams and goals. When you adopt the habit of becoming truly happy every day, everything good will naturally follow you. Over time, happiness can even become your default state. Try your best to follow the guidelines above, and I guarantee that you will start feeling happier immediately.

Chapter 29:
8 Ways To Gain Self-Confidence

Confidence is not something that can be inherited or learned but is rather a state of mind. Confidence is an attribute that most people would kill to possess. It comes from the feelings of well-being, acceptance of your body and mind (your self-esteem), and belief in your ability, skills, and experience. Positive thinking, knowledge, training, and talking to other people are valuable ways to help improve or boost your confidence levels. Although the definition of self-confidence is different for everyone, the simplest one can be 'to have faith and believe in yourself.'

Here are 8 Ways To Gain More Self-Confidence:

1. Look at what you have already achieved:

It's easy to lose confidence when we dwell on our past mistakes and believe that we haven't actually achieved anything yet. It's common to degrade ourselves and not see our achievements as something special. But we should be proud of ourselves even if we do just a single task throughout the day that benefited us or the society in any way. Please make a list of all the things you are proud of, and it can be as small as cleaning your room or as big as getting a good grade or excelling in your job. Keep adding your small or significant achievements every day. Whenever you feel low in confidence, pull out the list and remind yourself how far you have come, how many amazing things you have done, and how far you still have to go.

2. Polish the things you're already good at:

We feel confident in the things we know we are good at. Everyone has some kind of strengths, talents, and skills. You just have to recognize what's yours and work towards it to polish it. Some people are naturally good at everything they do. But that doesn't make you any less unique. You have to try to build on those things that you are good at, and they will help you built confidence in your abilities.

3. Set goals for yourself daily:

Whether it's cooking for yourself, reading a book, studying for a test, planning to meet a friend, or doing anything job-related, make a to-do list for yourself daily. Plan the steps that you have to take to achieve them. They don't necessarily have to be big goals; you should always aim for small achievements. At the end of the day, tick off all the things you did. This will help you gain confidence in your ability to get things done and give you a sense of self-appreciation and self-worth.

4. Talk yourself up:

That tiny voice inside of our heads is the key player in the game of our lives. You'll always be running low on confidence if that voice constantly has negative commentary in your mind telling you that you're not good enough. You should sit somewhere calm and quiet and talk to yourself out of all the negative things. Treat yourself like you would treat a loved one when they tend to feel down. Convince yourself that you can achieve anything, and there's nothing that can stop you. Fill your mind with positive thoughts and act on them.

5. Get a hobby:

Find yourself something that really interests you. It can either be photography, baking, writing, reading, anything at all. When you have found yourself something you are passionate about, commit yourself to it and give it a go. Chances are, you will get motivated and build skills more quickly; this will help you gain self-confidence as you would gradually get better at it and feel accomplished. The praises you will get for it will also boost your confidence.

6. Face your fears:

The best way to gain confidence is to face your fears head-on. There's no time to apply for a promotion or ask someone out on a date until you feel confident enough. Practice facing your fears even if it means that you will embarrass yourself or mess up. Remind yourself that it's just an experiment. You might learn that making mistakes or being anxious isn't half as bad as you would have thought. It will help you gain confidence each time you move forward, and it will prevent you from taking any risks that will result in negative consequences.

7. Surround yourself with positive people:

Observe your friends and the people around you. Do they lift you and accept who you are or bring you down and point out your flaws? A man is known by the company he keeps. Your friends should always positively influence your thoughts and attitude and make you feel better about yourself.

8. **Learn To Strike A Balance:**

Self-confidence is not a static measure. Some days, we might feel more confident than others. We might often feel a lack of confidence due to criticism, failures, lack of knowledge, or low self-esteem. While another time we might feel over-confident. We might come off as arrogant and self-centred to other people, and it can eventually lead to our failure. We should keep a suitable amount of confidence within ourselves.

Conclusion:

Confidence is primarily the result of how we have been taught and brought up. We usually learn from others how to behave and what to think of ourselves. Confidence is also a result of our experiences and how we learn to react in different situations. Everyone struggles with confidence issues at one time or another, but these quick fixes should enough to boost your confidence. Start with the easier targets, and then work yourself up. I believe in you. Always!

Chapter 30:

8 Ways To Love Yourself First

"Your task is not to seek for love, but merely to seek and find all the barriers within yourself that you have built against it." - Rumi.

Most of us are so busy waiting for someone to come into our lives and love us that we have forgotten about the one person we need to love the most – ourselves. Most psychologists agree that being loved and being able to love is crucial to our happiness. As quoted by Sigmund Freud, "love and work … work and love. That's all there is." It is the mere relationship of us with ourselves that sets the foundation for all other relationships and reveals if we will have a healthy relationship or a toxic one.

Here are some tips on loving yourself first before searching for any kind of love in your life.

1. Know That Self-Love Is Beautiful

Don't ever consider self-love as being narcissistic or selfish, and these are two completely different things. Self-love is rather having positive regard for our wellbeing and happiness. When we adopt self-love, we see higher levels of self-esteem within ourselves, are less critical and harsh with ourselves while making mistakes, and can celebrate our positive qualities and accept all our negative ones.

2. **Always be kind to yourself:**

We are humans, and humans are tended to get subjected to hurts, shortcomings, and emotional pain. Even if our family, friends, or even our partners may berate us about our inadequacies, we must learn to accept ourselves with all our imperfections and flaws. We look for acceptance from others and be harsh on ourselves if they tend to be cruel or heartless with us. We should always focus on our many positive qualities, strengths, and abilities, and admirable traits; rather than harsh judgments, comparisons, and self-hatred get to us. Always be gentle with yourself.

3. **Be the love you feel within yourself:**

You may experience both self-love and self-hatred over time. But it would be best if you always tried to focus on self-love more. Try loving yourself and having positive affirmations. Do a love-kindness meditation or spiritual practices to nourish your soul, and it will help you feel love and compassion toward yourself. Try to be in that place of love throughout your day and infuse this love with whatever interaction you have with others.

4. **Give yourself a break:**

We don't constantly live in a good phase. No one is perfect, including ourselves. It's okay to not be at the top of your game every day, or be happy all the time, or love yourself always, or live without pain. Excuse your bad days and embrace all your imperfections and mistakes. Accept your negative emotions but don't let them overwhelm you. Don't set high standards for yourself, both emotionally and mentally. Don't judge yourself for whatever you feel, and always embrace your emotions wholeheartedly.

5. Embrace yourself:

Are you content to sit all alone because the feelings of anxiety, fear, guilt, or judgment will overwhelm you? Then you have to practice being comfortable in your skin. Go within and seek solace in yourself, practice moments of alone time and observe how you treat yourself. Allow yourself to be mindful of your beliefs, feelings, and thoughts, and embrace solitude. The process of loving yourself starts with understanding your true nature.

6. Be grateful:

Rhonda Bryne, the author of The Magic, advises, "When you are grateful for the things you have, no matter how small they may be, you will see those things instantly increase." Look around you and see all the things that you are blessed to have. Practice gratitude daily and be thankful for all the things, no matter how good or bad they are. You will immediately start loving yourself once you realize how much you have to be grateful for.

7. Be helpful to those around you:

You open the door for divine love the moment you decide to be kind and compassionate toward others. "I slept and dreamt that life was a joy. I awoke and saw that life was service. I acted, and behold, and service was a joy." - Rabindranath Tagore. The love and positive vibes that you wish upon others and send out to others will always find a way back to you. Your soul tends to rejoice when you are kind, considerate, and compassionate. You have achieved the highest form of self-love when you decide to serve others. By helping others, you will realize that you don't need someone else to feel complete; you are complete. It will help you feel more love and fulfillment in your life.

8. Do things you enjoy doing:

If you find yourself stuck in a monotonous loop, try to get some time out for yourself and do the things that you love. There must be a lot of hobbies and passions that you might have put a brake on. Dust them off and start doing them again. Whether it's playing any sport, learning a new skill, reading a new book, writing in on your journal, or simply cooking or baking for yourself, start doing it again. We shouldn't compromise on the things that make us feel alive. Doing the things we enjoy always makes us feel better about ourselves and boost our confidence.

Conclusion:

Loving yourself is nothing short of a challenge. It is crucial for your emotional health and ability to reach your best potential. But the good news is, we all have it within us to believe in ourselves and live the best life we possibly can. Find what you are passionate about, appreciate yourself, and be grateful for what's in your life. Accept yourself as it is.

Chapter 31:
9 Tips on How To Have A Strong Relationship

Who doesn't want a strong relationship? Everyone wants to have that high-level understanding with their partner that lasts a lifetime. It is scientifically proven that people who are in healthy relationships have less stress and more happiness.

Healthy relationship not only helps us increase our overall feelings of happiness, but stress-reduction also helps us improve our overall quality of physical and mental health that make every-day life more pleasing to go through. Relationships can be in the form of family, work, friendships, and also romantic ones. Depending on the area that matters the most to you at this very point in your life, you can choose to focus on that specific one until you feel you are ready to focus on the next.

If building powerful relationships is a priority of yours as it is mine, then stay with me till the end of this video because we will be discussing **9 Magical** Tips on How To Have A Strong Relationship with whoever you want. Let's Begin.

Number one
Listen to Each Other
This is the first and probably the most important thing that you might want to take note of. Just think, how many arguments have you had that

went in the wrong direction just because no one was willing to simply just listen? In order to understand each other's point of view both parties must be willing to open up their ears instead of their mouths first. You need to have the stamina to listen to their side of the story before airing yours.

If you truly want a healthy relationship then the foundations starts with a good listening ear. To listen not only when the other party have problems in their lives, but also when they have a problem with you. Develop a good sense of compassion and empathy in the process.

Bitter thoughts, grudge-holding, and negativity toward the other person only serve to weaken your relationships, not strengthen them. So try to understand each other, let the other person speak, and then sort things out in the best possible way.

Number two
Give Time For The Relationship To Grow

For any relationship to truly blossom, it is important to spend the necessary quality time together. Whether the relationship is with family members, friends, or lovers, it takes energy and effort nonetheless. Any amount of energy you spend on that person will reap its benefits later. Now, I am not saying to drastically change your life or to go on adventures or expensive dates to make your relationship healthy. All you have to do is simply get yourself free for a day or night once a week and do something different together, like having a date night, playing games, cooking and eating, watching movies or whatever you like, just give your best at that time. Be present with them and don't be distracted checking your phone or replying work messages.

Number three
Give Time To Yourself

Now I needed to talk about this one right after the number two. I think a good relationship should be balanced. In the previous point, I talked about spending quality time in relationships, but I also don't mean that you should give all your energy to them or stop doing things that energizes your soul. Don't sacrifice your own hobbies for the sake of others. I agree that you need to take more initiative in relationships but at the same time you need to take care of your own happiness too. So give time to yourself and spend it doing things that fills your soul with happiness and gratefulness. You will feel recharged and fresh as a result when you engage in your relationships.

Number four
Learn To Appreciate Little Things

This point will touch more on the romantic relationship side of things. If you are in a relationship for quite a while then there is a chance that you might get complacent and too comfortable. You might also gradually forget the little things that make the person special. As a result the other person could potentially feel like you may be taking them for granted. To avoid this, you need to start making it a constant reminder to yourself to appreciate the little things your partner does for you. Say "I love you" to them, give cute little gifts, give them surprises and tell them how much they mean to you. You need to show your partner how much you love them so they never feel taken for granted. So yeah, start doing all this and make your bond strong!!

Number five
Learn To Forgive

It is well said, "relationships require a lot of forgiveness". As I mentioned earlier, bitter thoughts and grudge-holding just hurt your relationship in the long run. So if you want a happy relationship then you should learn to forgive. If there is something on your mind that your partner did and you can't forget then sit and talk to them about it and try to come up with a good solution. If any of you makes any mistake, you should forgive them with a smiling face and tell them that these little mistakes can't lessen your love. Work on yourself, make your heart ready for what you see coming and even what you don't see coming, and let things go in the right direction. You need to make your heart learn to forgive, this is the only key.

Number Six
Don't expect your partner to complete you

You should be confident about whatever you have. If you are looking for a healthy relationship then you should not expect your partner to complete you. Sometimes, we expect things from our partners which we lack and it can put a strain on your relationship. What you could do instead is to constantly work on yourself to the point that you feel you truly and rightfully deserving of every good thing that comes your way. That you feel secure and independent at the same time in the relationship. Loving yourself first goes a long way in maintaining a strong and healthy relationship with others.

Number Seven
Ways Of Showing Love

Different people show and receive love in their own unique ways. Understanding how the other party expresses or receives love is the key to building a strong relationship. Some people do it by caring for you while others express it through physical affection like hugs and kisses. If you don't know that the specific love language is between you and the other party then it might cause problems in the long run. To really ensure the other party feels loved you have to express it in the way that they receive the most strongly. Go find out what they are by asking them and then start giving it right away!

Number eight
Be Flexible

If you want a healthy relationship then you have to learn to be flexible as well. Flexible in the face of any changes that might occur in your relationship. It is a known fact that change is the only constant in life. We may never be prepared but we should do our best to adapt to new situations that we may find ourselves in. It is also therefore unrealistic not to expect our relationships to change as time progresses as well. Learn to adapt and grow in this new stage and you will be all the more happier for it.

Number nine
Make Decisions Jointly

A good and healthy relationship requires listening to each others' desires and concerns. While you may not always love to do the things that the other party wants, you should always try to find a compromise that suits both of your needs. Instead of insisting and making decisions all the time, try making decisions together that both of you will find enjoyable. Be it where to hang out, what to eat for a meal, where to go on a trip together, or even what kinds of products to buy for your home, make sure that the other party's points of view is heard so that they don't end up resenting you over the long run.